Phonics Screening Check Ages 5–6

National Test

KS1 Year1

Three complete checks with detailed advice

Published in the UK by Scholastic, 2018
Scholastic Distribution Centre, Bosworth Avenue, Tournament Fields, Warwick, CV34 6UQ
Scholastic Ireland, 89E Lagan Road, Dublin Industrial Estate, Glasnevin, Dublin, D11 HP5F

SCHOLASTIC and associated logos are trademarks and/or registered trademarks of Scholastic Inc.

www.scholastic.co.uk

© 2018 Scholastic

5 6 7 8 9 10 11 12   3 4 5 6 7 8 9 0 1 2

A CIP catalogue record for this book is available from the British Library.

ISBN 978-1407-18308-4

Printed and bound by Bell and Bain Ltd, Glasgow.
Paper made from wood grown in sustainable forests and other controlled sources.

Authors

Wendy Jolliffe and John Bennett

Editorial team

Kate Baxter, Tracey Cowell, Vicky Butt, Rachel Morgan, Melissa Somers

Design team

Sarah Garbett, Andrea Lewis, Shelley Best

Typesetting

Ricky Capanni, International Book Management

Illustration

Jim Peacock

Acknowledgements

Extracts from Department for Education website © Crown Copyright. Reproduced under the terms of the Open Government Licence (OGL). www.nationalarchives.gov.uk/doc/open-government-licence/version/3/

Every effort has been made to trace copyright holders for the works reproduced in this publication, and the publishers apologise or any inadvertent omissions.

Phonics Screening Check

Contents	Page

About this book

This book provides you with practice materials to help support children with the phonics screening check.

There are three checks provided in this book and five copies of each answer sheet.

There is scoring guidance for each practice paper on pages 56–59.

If you are unsure about any of the terminology used as you are reading the material, please refer to the glossary of terms (on page 64).

About the phonics screening check

The purpose of the phonics screening check is to assess whether children have achieved the age-expected level of understanding of phonics as demonstrated by decoding words. Decoding requires the ability to apply knowledge of letter–sound relationships to read written words. Based on a range of research into the teaching of reading, the Government requires that all children should learn phonics systematically as the prime approach to decoding. Phonics should be taught alongside a language-rich curriculum, which emphasises the importance of teaching other reading skills to support reading for meaning and pleasure. In 2012, a statutory requirement was introduced for children towards the end of Year 1 (usually aged 6) to have their phonic knowledge and understanding screened. For those children not achieving the expected level, the aim is for schools to provide additional support, as intervention at an early stage is effective in helping children to achieve good literacy skills.

Structure of the practice checks

The materials in this pack have been created following the principles of the Standards and Testing Agency (STA) screening checks. Every attempt has been made to ensure they are compatible with the national checks and will provide useful practice for children before they undertake the phonics screening check.

Using the practice checks

The practice checks can be used in the same way as you would use other practice materials. However, as the child is only aged five or six it is important to present the checks in a fun way that does not make them feel anxious. Full details about carrying out the checks are outlined below. Each practice paper contains 40 words, divided into two sections of 20 words. Both of the sections contain a mixture of real and pseudo (made-up) words. Section 1 contains 12 pseudo words and 8 real words and Section 2 has 8 pseudo words and 12 real words.

Pseudo words

The pseudo words are designed to assess children's ability to know the corresponding phonemes (or sounds) for the graphemes (letters), but also to be able to blend these into whole units or words. The ability to blend sounds together is a crucial skill in reading and therefore both aspects need to be assessed. A child may read some words by sight because they are familiar to them. Reading pseudo words will test the skill of blending (or combining) sounds in order to decode words more accurately. For example, reading 'groiks' and 'snemp' (examples of pseudo words) relies on your ability to put corresponding sounds to the letters and then blend them into a word, in other words, it is a pure test of your phonic knowledge.

The pseudo words should be introduced to children as names of imaginary creatures. There is a picture next to each pseudo word and children can be told that the word is the name of that type of creature. This should help children understand that the pseudo words should not be matched to their existing vocabulary. It is important to practise reading pseudo words and ensure that children know they are not real words. To prepare for the practice checks, you may like to play games with nonsense words. For ideas, see the section on supporting activities (pages 61–63).

What is in each section?

Section 1 of each screening check contains words with a simple structure – words where each letter is sounded out and which include common consonant and vowel combinations.

Section 2 has a variety of more complex structures, such as words which contain blends of three consonants and/or a split digraph (a sound that is represented by two letters and split by a consonant, for example 'scr**a**p**e**'), or words with trigraphs (three letters representing one sound, for example 'f**air**').

You may find the phoneme lists on the next two pages useful for reference.

Phoneme lists

The phoneme lists on the next two pages show the consonant and vowel phonemes which children should have learned prior to the phonic screening check.

The phonemes are listed alphabetically (for ease of reference), which may not reflect the order in which they are usually taught at school.

This is the list for consonant phonemes, vowel phonemes can be found on page 7.

Consonant phonemes	International phonetic alphabet symbol	Common spellings
/b/	b	**b**aby, ca**bb**age
/c/ /k/	k	**c**at, **Ch**ris, **k**ing, lu**ck**, **q**ueen
/ch/	tʃ	**ch**ip, wa**tch**
/d/	d	**d**og, pu**dd**le
/f/	f	**f**ish, **ph**oto, cof**f**ee
/g/	g	**g**ame, e**gg**
/h/	h	**h**at
/j/	dʒ	**j**ug, ju**dge**, **g**iant, bar**ge**
/l/	l	**l**eg, spe**ll**
/m/	m	**m**an, ha**mm**er, co**mb**
/ng/	ŋ	ri**ng**, si**nk**
/n/	n	**n**oise, **kn**ife, **gn**at
/p/	p	**p**aper, hi**pp**o
/r/	r	**r**abbit, **wr**ong, be**rr**y
/s/	s	**s**un, mou**se**, **c**ity, me**ss**, **sc**ience, mi**ce**
/sh/	ʃ	**sh**ip, mi**ss**ion, **ch**ef
/t/	t	**t**ap, be**tt**er
/th/	θ	**th**in
/th/	ð	**th**en
/v/	v	**v**an, dri**ve**
/w/	w	**w**ater, **wh**eel, q**u**een
/y/	j	**y**es
/z/	z	**z**ebra, plea**se**, i**s**, fi**zz**y, snee**ze**

SCHOLASTIC Practice for Phonics Screening Check

This is the list for vowel phonemes, consonant phonemes can be found on page 6.

Vowel phonemes	International phonetic alphabet symbol	Common spellings
/a/	æ	**a**pple
/ae/	eɪ	pl**ay**, t**a**ke, sn**ai**l, b**a**by
/air/	ɛə	h**air**, b**ear**, sh**are**
/ar/	ɑː	c**ar**, f**a**st (regional)
/au/	ɔː	s**au**ce, h**or**n, d**oor**, w**ar**n, cl**aw**, b**a**ll
/e/	e	**e**gg, br**ea**d
/ee/	iː	f**ee**l, h**ea**t, m**e**
/er/	ə	teach**er**, coll**ar**, doct**or**, **a**bout
/i/	ɪ	**i**nk, buck**e**t
/ie/	aɪ	t**ie**, f**igh**t, m**y**, b**i**ke, t**i**ger
/o/	ɒ	**o**ctopus, w**a**nt
/oe/	əʊ	fl**oa**t, sl**ow**, st**o**ne, n**o**se
/oi/	ɔɪ	c**oi**n, b**oy**
/ow/	aʊ	c**ow**, l**ou**d
/u/	ʌ	**u**mbrella, l**o**ve,
/u/	ʊ	t**oo**k, c**ou**ld, p**u**t
/ue/	uː	r**oo**m, cl**ue**, gr**ew**, t**u**ne
/ur/	ɜː	f**ur**, g**ir**l, t**er**m, h**ear**d, w**or**k

What the children should know before undertaking the check

To succeed in the screening check, children need to:

- have a thorough knowledge of the letters of the alphabet
- be able to hear and discriminate individual sounds in words and be able to manipulate these sounds
- be confident about the correspondence between approximately 44 phonemes (or sounds) in English and the graphemes (or letters) that represent them
- have an increasingly fast ability to link letters to sounds
- be able to break up words into common letter strings (combinations) or groups
- be confident in blending phonemes using correct pronunciation
- be able to break up multi-syllabic words into syllables and then into phonemes to blend into a word.

Detailed phonic knowledge

The expectation for competence in phonics by the end of Year 1 is that children should be able to decode **all** words (and pseudo words) containing:

- simple structures where each letter is sounded and with consonant digraphs (such as 'clap')
- two consonants together and a vowel (such as CVCC 'bend' or CCVC 'stop').

Children should also be able to decode **most** words (and pseudo words) containing:

- frequent vowel digraphs (such as 'pl**ay**')
- a single consonant string (such as '**cl**ip')
- two consonant strings and a vowel (such as CCVCC 'clump').

In addition, children should be able to decode **some** words (and pseudo words) containing:

- less frequent vowel digraphs and split digraphs (such as 'scr**ew**' and 't**u**n**e**')
- a single three-consonant string (such as '**str**ap')
- two syllables (such as 'cab/in').

How to carry out a check

An adult (often a teacher) who knows the child should work through the check with each child individually. The child's response to each word should be recorded on the answer sheet by ticking 'Correct' or 'Incorrect'. The adult should insert text in the 'Comment' column against incorrect answers, for example if a child read some sounds correctly, but not all, or if they tried to say a real word instead of a pseudo word. The adult can point to whole words, but should not point in a way which supports the decoding of the word.

Each check includes two practice pages comprising four real words on one page and four pseudo words on the other. These are provided to familiarise the child with the task. If a child struggles with the practice pseudo words, consider if it is appropriate to continue the check. (If you are a parent/carer, you may want to consult the child's teacher.)

The following statements/questions may be useful when working through the check with a child.

- 'I am going to ask you to read some words aloud.'
- 'Some of these words will be new and some you will have seen before.'
- 'Try to read each word, but don't worry if you can't manage some. You may find it helps to sound out the letters before reading the words.'
- 'We will start with some practice words which give you an idea of what the words look like.'
- 'Have a go at reading these words, which you should have seen before.'
- 'These words are not real words. They are names of imaginary creatures. You can see a picture of the creature next to each word.'
- 'Please can you read out the words on this page for me?'
- 'Now you are going to read the words and I am going to write down what you say on my sheet.'
- There are four words on each page. I will tell you at the start of each page whether they are real words that you may have seen before or whether they are names of imaginary creatures.'
- 'Are you ready to start reading the words to me?'

What to do if a child is struggling to complete a check

Most children should be able to attempt all the words in a check.

If a child is struggling, consider whether it is best to stop the check – it is important that they do not get upset when doing it. If a child shows signs of being tired, a rest break may be helpful once they reach the end of a page. If frequent breaks are needed, it may be best to stop the check completely.

Phonics Screening Check

Check 1

on

it

dog

gum

Practice sheet: pseudo words

ob

vad

isk

uct

Section 1

pab

vas

yon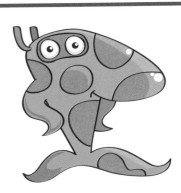

ilt

SCHOLASTIC Practice for Phonics Screening Check

tesh

chan

poin

chack

stip

prool

darps

thand

shin

buzz

harp

third

clip

track

pump

curls

Section 2

haim

yite

bigh

dirst

SCHOLASTIC Practice for Phonics Screening Check

flads

graiks

stramp

splew

moat

shape

hair

crate

slept

shrimp

scrub

strike

indeed

ending

perfect

thinking

Phonics Screening Check

Check 2

Practice sheet: real words

if

as

cat

run

Practice sheet: pseudo words

og

vab

usk

ilt

Section 1

peb

vup

yod

ult

besh

cham

poid

quock

SCHOLASTIC Practice for Phonics Screening Check

stid

proot

garps

thelk

chin

miss

lard

chirp

clap

trick

lump

girls

Section 1

bip

vut

jop

olt

lesh

cheg

noil

quish

stib

prook

jarps

thelp

SCHOLASTIC Practice for Phonics Screening Check

chap

fizz

horn

shirt

club

brick

limp

cards

Section 2

paim

hine

jigh

lirst

SCHOLASTIC Practice for Phonics Screening Check

flobs

broiks

strint

spraw

coat

shake

high

bride

■SCHOLASTIC Practice for Phonics Screening Check

trust

shrunk

strip

spray

upset

contain

feeling

target

Scoring guidance, further support and answer sheets

Scoring guidance

Answer sheets

The answer sheets can be found on pages 65–79. They can be cut out of the book so that you can use them to make notes as your child completes the check. There are five copies provided for each check.

Remember the following points when marking the check.

- Using the answer sheet, record one point for each word read correctly.
- Children may sound out phonemes before reading the word, but this is optional.
- Children may stretch or elongate the phonemes, if this is helpful or if they have been taught to do this at school. This is acceptable as long as they blend them correctly to pronounce the word.
- Alternative pronunciations should be considered for pseudo words if they are possible phonically (see the Notes on pronunciation section below).
- A child's accent should be taken into account and not disadvantage them. Similarly, if the child has speech difficulties, for example when pronouncing 'th', this should be considered.
- If a child makes an incorrect attempt but then corrects it, the word should be marked as correct.
- The adult should not say whether the child has read a word correctly but just encourage them to complete the task.
- A child should be given as long as required to read a word, although ten seconds is usually sufficient.
- In all, a check should take between four and nine minutes to complete.
- The three checks should not take place one after the other – or on the same day.

Notes on pronunciation

When decoding a real word in the screening check, the child must select the correct phoneme for the word in order to obtain a mark. For example the 'ow' in 'blow' should not be pronounced as the 'ow' in 'cow'.

However, **when decoding a pseudo word**, the child may use any plausible pronunciation. The tables on the next three pages provide guidance on the acceptable pronunciations of the pseudo words in the screening checks.

What the total score means

A child who scores 32 or more in this test could be considered to be meeting the expected standard, but please be aware that national standards change over time and these practice tests just provide an indicator of a child's ability.

Check 1: Acceptable pronunciations of pseudo words

Section 1

Pseudo word	Acceptable pronunciations	Phonemic representation
pab	This item uses the 'p' from 'pig' and rhymes with 'cab'.	/pæb/
vas	This item uses the 'v' from 'van' and rhymes with 'has'.	/væs/ or /væz/
yon	This item uses the 'y' from 'yes' and rhymes with 'don'.	/jɒn/
ilt	This item uses the 'i' from 'ill' and rhymes with 'kilt'.	/ɪlt/
tesh	This item uses the 't' from 'task' and rhymes with 'mesh'.	/tɛʃ/
chan	This item uses the 'ch' from 'change' and rhymes with 'tan'.	/tʃæn/
poin	This item uses the 'p' from 'point' and rhymes with 'coin'.	/pɔɪn/
chack	This item uses the 'ch' from 'chap' and rhymes with 'back'.	/tʃæk/
stip	This item uses the 'st' from 'still' and rhymes with 'tip'.	/stɪp/
prool	This item uses the 'pr' from 'proof' and rhymes with 'cool'. Regional pronunciations of 'oo' are acceptable.	/pru:l/ or /prʊl/
darps	This item uses the 'd' from 'dark' and rhymes with 'harps'.	/dɑ:ps/
thand	This item uses either the 'th' from 'this' or the 'th' from 'thin' and rhymes with 'sand'.	/ðænd/ or /θænd/

Section 2

Pseudo word	Acceptable pronunciations	Phonemic representation
haim	This item uses the 'h' from 'hail' and rhymes with 'aim'.	/heɪm/
yite	This item uses the 'y' from 'yes' and rhymes with 'kite'.	/yaɪt/
bigh	This item uses the 'b' from 'back' and rhymes with 'high'.	/baɪ/
dirst	This item uses the 'd' from 'dirt' and rhymes with 'first'.	/dɜ:st/
flads	This item uses the 'fl' from 'flog' and rhymes with 'pads'.	/flædz/
graiks	This item uses the 'gr' from 'groin' and rhymes with 'makes'.	/greɪkz/
stramp	This item uses the 'str' from 'strong' and rhymes with 'ramp'.	/stræmp/
splew	This item uses the 'spl' from 'split' and rhymes with 'flew'.	/splu:/

Check 2: Acceptable pronunciations of pseudo words

Section 1

Pseudo word	Acceptable pronunciations	Phonemic representation
peb	This item uses the 'p' from 'pig' and rhymes with 'web'.	/pɛb/
vup	This item uses the 'v' from 'van' and rhymes with 'cup'.	/vʌp/ or /vʊp/
yod	This item uses the 'y' from 'yes' and rhymes with 'nod'.	/jɒd/
ult	This item uses the 'u' from 'up' and rhymes with 'cult'.	/ʌlt/ or /ʊlt/
besh	This item uses the 'b' from 'bent' and rhymes with 'mesh'.	/bɛʃ/
cham	This item uses the 'ch' from 'change' and rhymes with 'ham'.	/tʃæm/
poid	This item uses the 'p' from 'point' and rhymes with 'void'.	/pɔɪd/
quock	This item uses the 'qu' from 'queen' and rhymes with 'clock'.	/kwɒk/
stid	This item uses the 'st' from 'still' and rhymes with 'lid'.	/stɪd/
proot	This item uses the 'pr' from 'proof' and rhymes with 'root'. Regional pronunciations of 'oo' are acceptable.	/pruːt/ or /prʊt/
garps	This item uses the 'g' from 'garden' and rhymes with 'harps'.	/gɑːps/
thelk	This item uses either the 'th' from 'this' or the 'th' from 'thin' and rhymes with 'elk'.	/ðɛlk/ or /θɛlk/

Section 2

Pseudo word	Acceptable pronunciations	Phonemic representation
jaim	This item uses the 'j' from 'jail' and rhymes with 'aim'.	/jeɪm/
tibe	This item uses the 't' from 'tap' and rhymes with 'bribe'.	/taɪb/
figh	This item uses the 'f' from 'fan' and rhymes with 'high'.	/faɪ/
hirst	This item uses the 'h' from 'hip' and rhymes with 'first'.	/hɜːst/
flums	This item uses the 'fl' from 'flog' and rhymes with 'gums'.	/flʌmz/ or /flʊmz/
troiks	This item uses the 'tr' from 'train' and rhymes with 'hoicks'.	/trɔɪkz/
strant	This item uses the 'str' from 'strong' and rhymes with 'rant'.	/strænt/
splow	This item uses the 'spl' from 'split' and rhymes with 'cow' or 'blow'.	/splaʊ/ or /spləʊ/

Check 3: Acceptable pronunciations of pseudo words

Section 1

Pseudo word	Acceptable pronunciations	Phonemic representation
bip	This item uses the 'b' from 'bid' and rhymes with 'nip'.	/bɪp/
vut	This item uses the 'v' from 'van' and rhymes with 'put'.	/vʌt/ or /vʊt/
jop	This item uses the 'j' from 'jot' and rhymes with 'top'.	/jɒp/
olt	This item uses the 'o' from 'on' and rhymes with 'halt'.	/ɒlt/
lesh	This item uses the 'l' from 'lent' and rhymes with 'mesh'.	/lɛʃ/
cheg	This item uses the 'ch' from 'change' and rhymes with 'leg'.	/tʃɛg/
noil	This item uses the 'n' from 'nib' and rhymes with 'toil'.	/nɔɪl/
quish	This item uses the 'qu' from 'queen' and rhymes with 'fish'.	/kwɪʃ/
stib	This item uses the 'st' from 'still' and rhymes with 'nib'.	/stɪb/
prook	This item uses the 'pr' from 'proof' and rhymes with 'look'. Regional pronunciations of 'oo' are acceptable.	/pruːk/ or /prʊk/
jarps	This item uses the 'j' from 'jam' and rhymes with 'harps'.	/jɑːps/
thelp	This item uses either the 'th' from 'this' or the 'th' from 'thin' and rhymes with 'help'.	/ðɛlp/ or /θɛlp/

Section 2

Pseudo word	Acceptable pronunciations	Phonemic representation
paim	This item uses the 'p' from 'pail' and rhymes with 'aim'.	/peɪm/
hine	This item uses the 'h' from 'hat' and rhymes with 'line'.	/haɪn/
jigh	This item uses the 'j' from 'jam' and rhymes with 'high'.	/jaɪ/
lirst	This item uses the 'l' from 'lip' and rhymes with 'first'.	/lɜːst/
flobs	This item uses the 'fl' from 'flog' and rhymes with 'sobs'.	/flɒbz/
broiks	This item uses the 'br' from 'brain' and rhymes with 'hoicks'.	/brɔɪkz/
strint	This item uses the 'str' from 'strong' and rhymes with 'mint'.	/strɪnt/
spraw	This item uses the 'spr' from 'sprint' and rhymes with 'law'.	/sprɔː/

Providing additional support

It is important to decide what type of difficulties a child is having if they have not achieved the expected score in a check.

The following prompts may be helpful and are accompanied by suggestions for further support.

Difficulty	Suggested support
Accurately distinguishing phonemes and being able to manipulate them in different ways.	It may be necessary to check if there are any hearing problems. If not, the child needs lots of additional support to distinguish different sounds. Playing games involving rhymes or alliteration is likely to be effective.
General language difficulties, such as limited vocabulary.	The child may have specific difficulties that need support from a specialist, making this screening check inappropriate for them at this stage. If in doubt, seek expert advice.
Blending phonemes into words.	Practise blending using books made up of words that are decodable at a child's phonic level. They are available alongside many phonic programmes. You can also practise blending using 'robot talk' (see the activity on page 61).
More difficult words in Section 2, such as long-vowel sounds or less common spellings for sounds.	Check that the child has a good knowledge of the correspondence between approximately 44 graphemes and the sounds they make, using a progress tracker available with many phonics schemes. If a child's recall of letters and sounds is limited, make use of multi-sensory approaches (see the guidance on page 62).
Blending two or three consonants (recalling three or more sounds).	It may help to undertake activities where words are broken down gradually (for example, for words like 'stand' you could encourage the child to chunk the word into 'st' and then to blend 'and', then put these together to form 'stand').
Problems with multi-syllabic words.	Check the child's ability to divide words into constituent syllables (see the activity on page 63).

Activities

Robot talk

'Robot talk' is helpful when practising segmenting and the reversible skill of blending phonemes. Children may be familiar with Daleks through the *Doctor Who* television programme. Hearing talk in a staccato way like a Dalek can be a useful way to begin to understand the idea of talking like a robot.

To begin a 'robot talk' activity with children, use a picture to show a robot who can only talk in phonemes. Below is an example of how you might undertake the activity. (Note: individual phonemes are separated with forward slashes to show that each phoneme should be said separately.)

Adult: 'This is Robbie. Because he is a robot he talks in a strange way – a bit like a Dalek. Let's hear him talk.'

               /s/a/d/ [Hold up the picture of a robot and pretend it is talking.]

               'What do you think he said? Can you repeat it?'

Child: 'Yes, /s/a/d/.'

Adult: 'What does he mean?'

Child: 'Is he sad?'

Adult: 'Well done! Yes, he says "sad".'

               'Now, he does not understand you unless you talk like a robot. You need to say the sounds – remember, we call them phonemes, separately. Shall we have a go? Let's try with pin.'

               'Good, it's /p/i/n/. Can you say that to Robbie? Let's see if he says it back to you.'

Child/'robot': /p/i/n/

Adult: 'Well done! Remember, when we talk to Robbie we must talk in phonemes.'

The activity could be adapted using a puppet who only speaks in phonemes.

Nonsense words for blending

Have fun making up nonsense words with children and link this to inventing stories about imaginary creatures. You might like to start with names such as bec, fet, mig, flads and cheg.

You can find a range of phonics interactive games and resources online.

Multi-sensory learning

The use of multi-sensory teaching methods can aid children's learning and retention of grapheme–phoneme correspondences.

These might include the use of:
- actions
- mnemonics
- songs/raps and rhymes
- visual prompts for each grapheme/phoneme correspondence.

Actions

Teach a different action for each sound. For example, for /**ai**/ have a hand cupped around your ear as if you are struggling to hear.

It is important to be consistent in teaching the same actions for a phoneme. Guidance from a particular scheme may be helpful, for example *Quick Fix for: Phonics* (Scholastic) or *Jolly Phonics* (Jolly Learning).

Mnemonics, songs/raps and rhymes

A saying or mnemonic can be accompanied by an action.

As phonemes are learned, sayings/mnemonics can be linked together to form a 'rap'. Said in a lively way, they can act as revision or overlearning of the phonemes taught and can be a fun way of learning.

When helping the child with a rap, it is important to follow these steps.

1. Say the phoneme twice /ay/ay/.

2. Say the mnemonic 'Play with hay'.

3. Say the letter names 'A Y'.

4. Do the corresponding action: lift pile of hay.

Visual prompts

The use of visual aids can support learning long-vowel phonemes. For instance, you can source images to fit the rap you create.

Multi-syllabic words

To read multi-syllabic words, it is important to start by breaking the word into syllables before further breaking it down into phonemes.

One useful and practical way to check how many syllables there are in a word is to place your hand flat horizontally beneath your chin and say a word. The number of times your chin drops (equivalent to the number of vowel phonemes in the word) denotes the number of syllables. Try this with a multi-syllabic word (for example, television is four syllables).

Have fun with clapping/beating/tapping out words or names, including with musical instruments. You can ask children to guess a name by beating or tapping a number of syllables (such as Pep/pa /Pig). You will probably need to restrict this exercise to well-known or famous characters and provide clues where appropriate.

Once children are confident at segmenting words into syllables, support them to break each syllable down into its constituent phonemes. Ensure that they know the difference between syllables and phonemes by talking about bigger chunks (syllables) and smaller parts of words (phonemes).

Here is an example for 'handbag'.

1. To check how many syllables are in the word (two), either tap out the syllables or place a hand horizontally underneath your chin and then say the word.

2. Segment 'hand' into phonemes: /h/ /a/ /n/ /d/.

3. Segment 'bag' into phonemes: /b/ /a/ /g/.

4. Blend both parts of the word to make 'handbag'.

Glossary of terms

Term	Meaning
Adjacent consonants	Consonants that appear next to each other in a word and that can be blended together, for example 'bl' in 'blip' and 'cr' in 'crisp'.
Alliteration	A sequence of words beginning with the same sound.
Blending	To draw individual sounds together to pronounce a word, such as /b/l/a/ck/ blended together to read 'black'.
CVC	A consonant-vowel-consonant combination in a word, often found in three-letter words such as 'cat', 'pin' or 'top'. You may also come across the abbreviation CCVC (consonant-consonant-vowel-consonant) for words such as 'clap' and 'from' and CVCC (consonant-vowel-consonant-consonant) for words such as 'mask' and 'belt'.
Digraph	Two letters which together make one sound, such as 'sh' in 'ship'. There are different types of digraph – vowel digraph (such as 'oi' in 'boil'), consonant digraph (such as 'ch' in 'church') and split digraph, (such as 'a–e' in 'late').
Graph	One letter that makes one sound.
Grapheme	Graphemes are the written representation of phonemes.
Grapheme–phoneme correspondence	A written representation of a phoneme; that is, a letter or group of letters representing a sound.
Item	A real word or pseudo word that a child is asked to read as part of the screening check.
Mnemonic	A device for remembering something, for example '/ee/ /ee/ feel the tree' for remembering the long /ee/ sound in 'tree'.
Phoneme	Phonemes are the smallest unit of speech sounds which make up a word. If you change a phoneme in a word, you would change its meaning. For example, there are three phonemes in the word 'sit': /s/ /i/ /t/. If you change the phoneme /s/ for /f/, you have a new word, 'fit'. If you change the phoneme /t/ in 'fit' for /sh/, you have a new word, 'fish': /f/ /i/ /sh/.
Pseudo word	A made-up word.
Segmenting	Splitting up a word into its individual phonemes in order to spell it, for example the word 'pat' has three phonemes: /p/a/t/.
Split digraph	Two letters which work as a pair to make one sound but are separated within the word by a consonant (such as 'o–e' in 'stove').
Syllable	A unit of pronunciation with one vowel sound.
Trigraph	Three letters representing one sound (such as he**dge**, h**air**, sna**tch**).

CHECK 1: Answer sheet

First name	
Last name	
Date	

Please tick the 'Correct' or 'Incorrect' box for each word and use the 'Total correct' box to record the final score. Use the 'Comment' box to note unacceptable attempts or to highlight where a word was not attempted.

Section 1					Section 2			
Word	**Correct**	**Incorrect**	**Comment**		**Word**	**Correct**	**Incorrect**	**Comment**
pab					haim			
vas					yite			
yon					bigh			
ilt					dirst			
tesh					flads			
chan					graiks			
poin					stramp			
chack					splew			
stip					moat			
prool					shape			
darps					hair			
thand					crate			
shin					slept			
buzz					shrimp			
harp					scrub			
third					strike			
clip					indeed			
track					ending			
pump					perfect			
curls					thinking			

Total correct	

CHECK 1: Answer sheet

First name	
Last name	
Date	

Please tick the 'Correct' or 'Incorrect' box for each word and use the 'Total correct' box to record the final score. Use the 'Comment' box to note unacceptable attempts or to highlight where a word was not attempted.

Section 1					Section 2			
Word	**Correct**	**Incorrect**	**Comment**		**Word**	**Correct**	**Incorrect**	**Comment**
pab					haim			
vas					yite			
yon					bigh			
ilt					dirst			
tesh					flads			
chan					graiks			
poin					stramp			
chack					splew			
stip					moat			
prool					shape			
darps					hair			
thand					crate			
shin					slept			
buzz					shrimp			
harp					scrub			
third					strike			
clip					indeed			
track					ending			
pump					perfect			
curls					thinking			

Total correct

CHECK 1: Answer sheet

First name	
Last name	
Date	

Please tick the 'Correct' or 'Incorrect' box for each word and use the 'Total correct' box to record the final score. Use the 'Comment' box to note unacceptable attempts or to highlight where a word was not attempted.

Section 1			
Word	**Correct**	**Incorrect**	**Comment**
pab			
vas			
yon			
ilt			
tesh			
chan			
poin			
chack			
stip			
prool			
darps			
thand			
shin			
buzz			
harp			
third			
clip			
track			
pump			
curls			

Section 2			
Word	**Correct**	**Incorrect**	**Comment**
haim			
yite			
bigh			
dirst			
flads			
graiks			
stramp			
splew			
moat			
shape			
hair			
crate			
slept			
shrimp			
scrub			
strike			
indeed			
ending			
perfect			
thinking			

Total correct	

CHECK 1: Answer sheet

First name	
Last name	
Date	

Please tick the 'Correct' or 'Incorrect' box for each word and use the 'Total correct' box to record the final score. Use the 'Comment' box to note unacceptable attempts or to highlight where a word was not attempted.

Section 1				Section 2			
Word	Correct	Incorrect	Comment	Word	Correct	Incorrect	Comment
pab				haim			
vas				yite			
yon				bigh			
ilt				dirst			
tesh				flads			
chan				graiks			
poin				stramp			
chack				splew			
stip				moat			
prool				shape			
darps				hair			
thand				crate			
shin				slept			
buzz				shrimp			
harp				scrub			
third				strike			
clip				indeed			
track				ending			
pump				perfect			
curls				thinking			

Total correct	

■SCHOLASTIC Practice for Phonics Screening Check

CHECK 1: Answer sheet

First name	
Last name	
Date	

Please tick the 'Correct' or 'Incorrect' box for each word and use the 'Total correct' box to record the final score. Use the 'Comment' box to note unacceptable attempts or to highlight where a word was not attempted.

Section 1			
Word	**Correct**	**Incorrect**	**Comment**
pab			
vas			
yon			
ilt			
tesh			
chan			
poin			
chack			
stip			
prool			
darps			
thand			
shin			
buzz			
harp			
third			
clip			
track			
pump			
curls			

Section 2			
Word	**Correct**	**Incorrect**	**Comment**
haim			
yite			
bigh			
dirst			
flads			
graiks			
stramp			
splew			
moat			
shape			
hair			
crate			
slept			
shrimp			
scrub			
strike			
indeed			
ending			
perfect			
thinking			
Total correct			

CHECK 2: Answer sheet

First name	
Last name	
Date	

Please tick the 'Correct' or 'Incorrect' box for each word and use the 'Total correct' box to record the final score. Use the 'Comment' box to note unacceptable attempts or to highlight where a word was not attempted.

Section 1				Section 2			
Word	**Correct**	**Incorrect**	**Comment**	**Word**	**Correct**	**Incorrect**	**Comment**
peb				jaim			
vup				tibe			
yod				figh			
ult				hirst			
besh				flums			
cham				troiks			
poid				strant			
quock				splow			
stid				coal			
proot				shade			
garps				pair			
thelk				flame			
chin				craft			
miss				shrink			
lard				strap			
chirp				screw			
clap				undid			
trick				window			
lump				sailing			
girls				servant			
				Total correct			

SCHOLASTIC Practice for Phonics Screening Check

CHECK 2: Answer sheet

First name	
Last name	
Date	

Please tick the 'Correct' or 'Incorrect' box for each word and use the 'Total correct' box to record the final score. Use the 'Comment' box to note unacceptable attempts or to highlight where a word was not attempted.

Section 1				Section 2			
Word	Correct	Incorrect	Comment	Word	Correct	Incorrect	Comment
peb				jaim			
vup				tibe			
yod				figh			
ult				hirst			
besh				flums			
cham				troiks			
poid				strant			
quock				splow			
stid				coal			
proot				shade			
garps				pair			
thelk				flame			
chin				craft			
miss				shrink			
lard				strap			
chirp				screw			
clap				undid			
trick				window			
lump				sailing			
girls				servant			

Total correct	

CHECK 2: Answer sheet

First name	
Last name	
Date	

Please tick the 'Correct' or 'Incorrect' box for each word and use the 'Total correct' box to record the final score. Use the 'Comment' box to note unacceptable attempts or to highlight where a word was not attempted.

Section 1				Section 2			
Word	**Correct**	**Incorrect**	**Comment**	**Word**	**Correct**	**Incorrect**	**Comment**
peb				jaim			
vup				tibe			
yod				figh			
ult				hirst			
besh				flums			
cham				troiks			
poid				strant			
quock				splow			
stid				coal			
proot				shade			
garps				pair			
thelk				flame			
chin				craft			
miss				shrink			
lard				strap			
chirp				screw			
clap				undid			
trick				window			
lump				sailing			
girls				servant			

Total correct	

SCHOLASTIC Practice for Phonics Screening Check

CHECK 2: Answer sheet

First name	
Last name	
Date	

Please tick the 'Correct' or 'Incorrect' box for each word and use the 'Total correct' box to record the final score. Use the 'Comment' box to note unacceptable attempts or to highlight where a word was not attempted.

Section 1					Section 2			
Word	**Correct**	**Incorrect**	**Comment**		**Word**	**Correct**	**Incorrect**	**Comment**
peb					jaim			
vup					tibe			
yod					figh			
ult					hirst			
besh					flums			
cham					troiks			
poid					strant			
quock					splow			
stid					coal			
proot					shade			
garps					pair			
thelk					flame			
chin					craft			
miss					shrink			
lard					strap			
chirp					screw			
clap					undid			
trick					window			
lump					sailing			
girls					servant			

Total correct

CHECK 2: Answer sheet

First name	
Last name	
Date	

Please tick the 'Correct' or 'Incorrect' box for each word and use the 'Total correct' box to record the final score. Use the 'Comment' box to note unacceptable attempts or to highlight where a word was not attempted.

Section 1				Section 2			
Word	**Correct**	**Incorrect**	**Comment**	**Word**	**Correct**	**Incorrect**	**Comment**
peb				jaim			
vup				tibe			
yod				figh			
ult				hirst			
besh				flums			
cham				troiks			
poid				strant			
quock				splow			
stid				coal			
proot				shade			
garps				pair			
thelk				flame			
chin				craft			
miss				shrink			
lard				strap			
chirp				screw			
clap				undid			
trick				window			
lump				sailing			
girls				servant			
				Total correct			

CHECK 3: Answer sheet

First name	
Last name	
Date	

Please tick the 'Correct' or 'Incorrect' box for each word and use the 'Total correct' box to record the final score. Use the 'Comment' box to note unacceptable attempts or to highlight where a word was not attempted.

Section 1			
Word	**Correct**	**Incorrect**	**Comment**
bip			
vut			
jop			
olt			
lesh			
cheg			
noil			
quish			
stib			
prook			
jarps			
thelp			
chap			
fizz			
horn			
shirt			
club			
brick			
limp			
cards			

Section 2			
Word	**Correct**	**Incorrect**	**Comment**
paim			
hine			
jigh			
lirst			
flobs			
broiks			
strint			
spraw			
coat			
shake			
high			
bride			
trust			
shrunk			
strip			
spray			
upset			
contain			
feeling			
target			

Total correct	

CHECK 3: Answer sheet

First name	
Last name	
Date	

Please tick the 'Correct' or 'Incorrect' box for each word and use the 'Total correct' box to record the final score. Use the 'Comment' box to note unacceptable attempts or to highlight where a word was not attempted.

Section 1				Section 2			
Word	**Correct**	**Incorrect**	**Comment**	**Word**	**Correct**	**Incorrect**	**Comment**
bip				paim			
vut				hine			
jop				jigh			
olt				lirst			
lesh				flobs			
cheg				broiks			
noil				strint			
quish				spraw			
stib				coat			
prook				shake			
jarps				high			
thelp				bride			
chap				trust			
fizz				shrunk			
horn				strip			
shirt				spray			
club				upset			
brick				contain			
limp				feeling			
cards				target			

Total correct	

CHECK 3: Answer sheet

First name	
Last name	
Date	

Please tick the 'Correct' or 'Incorrect' box for each word and use the 'Total correct' box to record the final score. Use the 'Comment' box to note unacceptable attempts or to highlight where a word was not attempted.

Section 1					Section 2			
Word	**Correct**	**Incorrect**	**Comment**		**Word**	**Correct**	**Incorrect**	**Comment**
bip					paim			
vut					hine			
jop					jigh			
olt					lirst			
lesh					flobs			
cheg					broiks			
noil					strint			
quish					spraw			
stib					coat			
prook					shake			
jarps					high			
thelp					bride			
chap					trust			
fizz					shrunk			
horn					strip			
shirt					spray			
club					upset			
brick					contain			
limp					feeling			
cards					target			

Total correct

CHECK 3: Answer sheet

First name	
Last name	
Date	

Please tick the 'Correct' or 'Incorrect' box for each word and use the 'Total correct' box to record the final score. Use the 'Comment' box to note unacceptable attempts or to highlight where a word was not attempted.

Section 1					Section 2			
Word	**Correct**	**Incorrect**	**Comment**		**Word**	**Correct**	**Incorrect**	**Comment**
bip					paim			
vut					hine			
jop					jigh			
olt					lirst			
lesh					flobs			
cheg					broiks			
noil					strint			
quish					spraw			
stib					coat			
prook					shake			
jarps					high			
thelp					bride			
chap					trust			
fizz					shrunk			
horn					strip			
shirt					spray			
club					upset			
brick					contain			
limp					feeling			
cards					target			

Total correct	

78

SCHOLASTIC Practice for Phonics Screening Check

CHECK 3: Answer sheet

First name	
Last name	
Date	

Please tick the 'Correct' or 'Incorrect' box for each word and use the 'Total correct' box to record the final score. Use the 'Comment' box to note unacceptable attempts or to highlight where a word was not attempted.

Section 1				Section 2			
Word	**Correct**	**Incorrect**	**Comment**	**Word**	**Correct**	**Incorrect**	**Comment**
bip				paim			
vut				hine			
jop				jigh			
olt				lirst			
lesh				flobs			
cheg				broiks			
noil				strint			
quish				spraw			
stib				coat			
prook				shake			
jarps				high			
thelp				bride			
chap				trust			
fizz				shrunk			
horn				strip			
shirt				spray			
club				upset			
brick				contain			
limp				feeling			
cards				target			

Total correct	

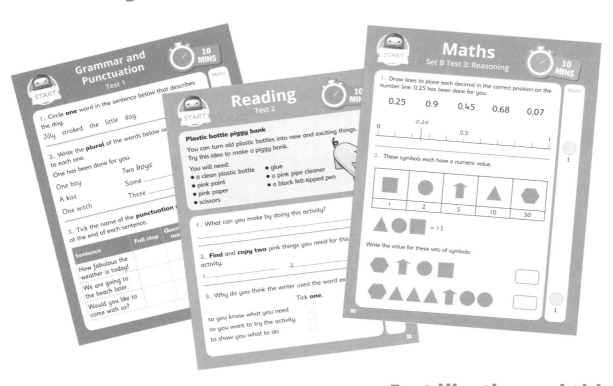